P9-AOR-992

BS
2595.6
.P5
N93
1990

JESUS' CLEAR CALL TO JUSTICE

DOROTHY YODER NYCE

GOSHEN COLLEGE LIBRARY
GOSHEN, INDIANA

HERALD PRESS
Scottdale, Pennsylvania
Waterloo, Ontario

Library of Congress Cataloging-in-Publication Data
Nyce, Dorothy Yoder.
    Jesus' clear call to justice / Dorothy Yoder Nyce.
      p. cm. — (Peace and justice series ; 11)
    Includes bibliographical references.
    ISBN 0-8361-3533-4 (alk. paper)
    1. Bible. N.T. Luke—Criticism, interpretation, etc.
  2. Peace-Biblical teaching. 3. Justice—Biblical teaching.
  4. Liberation theology. I. Title. II. Series.
  BS2595.6.P5N93 1990
  261.8—dc20   90-43599
                                                        CIP

The paper used in this publication is recycled and meets the minimum
requirements of American National Standard for Information
Sciences—Permanence of Paper for Printed Library Materials, ANSI
Z39.48-1984.

Scripture quotations are from the Revised Standard Version of
the Bible, copyright 1946, 1952, 1971 by the Division of
Christian Education of the National Council of the Churches
of Christ in the USA. Used by permission.

JESUS' CLEAR CALL TO JUSTICE
Copyright © 1990 by Herald Press, Scottdale, Pa. 15683
  Published simultaneously in Canada by Herald Press,
  Waterloo, Ont. N2L 6H7. All rights reserved.
Library of Congress Catalog Number: 90-43599
International Standard Book Number: 0-8361-3533-4
Printed in the United States of America
Book design by Gwen M. Stamm/Cover art by Merrill R. Miller

1 2 3 4 5 6 7 8 9 10 96 95 94 93 92 91 90

With thanks for resources which have most directly helped me to own Jesus' clear call to justice.

Film: "The Gospel According to St. Matthew" —Produced by Pasolini

Books: *Biblical Affirmations of Woman*
Texts of Terror
In Memory of Her
To Change the World

Scripture Teachers: Elisabeth Schüssler Fiorenza, Leonard Swidler, Robert McAfee Brown, Phyllis Trible, Josephine Ford, Mary Schertz, Rosemary Radford Ruether, Raymond Brown

Oppressed People: Marginalized women around the world

Contents

How Enemies, Justice, and Sin Shape
    Forgiveness
Forgiveness Against Odds
A Final Example

Foreword

You may be surprised to find a book on justice beginning with a chapter on peace. However, the biblical understanding of justice depends on the biblical concept of peace.

As the author notes, biblical peace combines meanings such as wholeness (salvation), completeness, total well-being, and the absence of injustice. Thus, peace lies at the heart of the gospel.

This peace centers not only on right relationship with God, but also on right relationships with others. Seen in this light, peace and justice are not teachings and actions that we ignore or obey as we may choose. Rather, they become primary concerns of the good news God offers to and through the Christian church.

The author also notes that Christians find a basis for justice-making in their understanding of God. To know God is to do justice (Jeremiah 22:16). Because of concern for justice, Christians will work for a new social order that is "stripped of sin," or the will to dominate. The concept of God's king-dom is discussed in broader terms: God's presence, order, and will.

Peace and justice for all marks this new order. Where relationships are marred, Christians will work toward forgiveness. The author explores a dozen texts—rooted in such occasions as table fellowship, anointing, adultery, and crucifixion—which highlight Jesus' commitment to forgiveness.

The author concludes each of the four chapters with an example of how a text can be retold within a given country of our world. These could be useful for reading or acting in worship settings.

This book is Volume 11 in a series on peace and justice listed inside the back cover. For more on the theme, check those sources.

—*J. Allen Brubaker, Editor*
Peace and Justice Series

Author's Preface

When invited to write for this series, I wondered how best to present the broad New Testament material on peace and justice themes. Convinced that the study should focus on the teaching and practice of Jesus, I chose Luke's story of the gospel.

I value disciplined study of Scripture. I wish to take texts seriously—to discover, as much as we human beings can, what Jesus meant about having eyes to truly see and ears to truly hear his words. I expect to find basic principles to live by. I do not expect Luke's stories merely to entertain me or bless comfortable living.

I expect Jesus' words and actions to evaluate—to confront wrong and defend right. We decide whether to close ourselves against Jesus' calls to change. Those with the will to apply the basics embedded in God's good news then meet daily issues in strength.

I could have used other texts. The more than forty[1] examined here offer both general and specific truth. They retell Jesus' teaching and show Jesus' untiring effort to broadcast God's message of wholeness (salvation) and inclusion. *I encourage you to read each biblical text along with the discussion.* To not read the texts is an injustice to the Author and this author. You might then reflect on how your experience adds insight or raises questions.

Concern to treat biblical content with integrity was central to my study. Also important was concern to explore new meanings and resources in order to assist and stir personal growth.

The conviction that making justice is a key expression of spirituality undergirds my work. To include "minority" people at my table is to live out prayer. To counter social forces that broaden economic or social gaps is to respond to God's Spirit acting within.

In other words, to refuse to extend privilege to a few but grant new dignity to people limited by society is to make truth practical. It puts into practice, "Thy will be done . . . forgive us our debts . . . deliver us from evil."

My work with biblical texts emerges from experience as a woman and as a person indebted to global friends. For decades, western Christians have not absorbed Jesus' radical insistence that the gospel *includes*, especially those often made marginal.

I recall a woman student's comment when I was her seminary teacher. After reading Leonard Swidler's section on Jesus and the gospels (in *Biblical Affirmation of Woman*), she said, "Now I understand grace!" Exploring that grace of Jesus the Advocate is one of my goals in this book.

Having lived in India has shaped my views and understandings. I have listened to women and men Bible teachers from India. I have read many books about social justice by Indian writers. And I have struggled with western privilege and oppression.

My desire is to credit non-western experience and people. My wish is to learn from them, to change because of the truth they teach me. I am not limited to listening only if they praise western Christian influence (which has often stifled their well-being). Instead, I choose to repent of our complicity in oppression.

The examples, based on biblical stories, which conclude each chapter grow out of global concern. I purposely focus each story in a two-thirds world setting.

Lois Barrett's first book in this series, *The Way God Fights*, is helpful background to this volume. A survey of war and peace in the Old Testament, it treats the Hebrew concept of *shalom*. Both the Hebrew word *shalom* and the Greek word *eirene* translate into the English word *peace*. Both have the primary meaning of wholeness or completeness.

Being at peace and experiencing justice are central to the biblical principle of wholeness or salvation. Well-being, nonviolence, harmony, and empowerment also describe it. Both God-human and person-to-person relationships are involved. Bruce C. Birch suggests, "Concern for peace must place our opposition to war alongside an equal concern for every enemy of well-being and wholeness: injustice, oppression, exploitation, disease, famine."[2]

Peace is the absence of injustice. And *justice* includes understanding the will and character of God. Therefore, I was drawn to the theological term *kingdom* which means the presence, will, or order of God. Central to this eternal order is discipleship. Disciples are loyal, empowered people who show their faith in God by empowering others.

When human beings fail, God's faithfulness or justice is known in part through *forgiveness*. Jesus repeatedly lived that out. With compassion, he confronted both secular and religious people who chose to avoid the clear call to justice. With compassion, he also comforted the afflicted and blessed those who forgave.

Two groups deserve thanks for interacting with earlier drafts of the book: the Harlan Mennonite Fellowship in Kentucky, and the 1988 Mennonite Board of Missions Overseas Seminar group which met in Goshen, Indiana.

CHAPTER 1

Peace, or Well-Being

The New Testament understanding of peace grows out of the Old Testament's use of *shalom*. This Hebrew concept sees peace as encompassing well-being for all—people, land, all created life. God blesses all. God wishes wholeness for all.

Many desire peace. True peace would include: ample resources untouched by violence or disaster. Friendship and mutual empowerment. Freedom from enemies. Sustained justice. Union or wholeness with God.[3]

But the world has yet to achieve true peace. Yes, the journey toward wholeness has begun. But it is blocked in many ways. Several questions occur. Will peace ever be complete in this life? If not, will we praise partial but positive efforts for peace?

Does knowing the goal motivate or discourage us? Perhaps both. Understanding peace can prompt renewed commitment to its presence in our world.

Using texts from Luke, this chapter looks at peace as a *greeting*, a *path*, and a *response to faith*.

Then it examines discord, such as the Samaritan-Jewish conflict and divisions within family or religious settings. Compared to Old Testament usage, Luke says little about warfare. He does, however, present brief accounts of swords and warnings of future persecution.

Peace as Path, Greeting, or Response to Faith

When able to speak (after being temporarily struck dumb), Zechariah sang about the coming day that would "guide our feet into the way of peace" (Luke 1:79). People expected the Messiah to bless God's chosen ones with earthly peace, meaning safety or salvation. The "way of peace"—or forgiveness and reconciliation with God—would extend God's presence.

Thanks to that presence, the angels praised God for peace [or salvation] and good will on earth (Luke 2:14). Jesus' coming made possible true peace with God. This peace was more than absence of war on land or sea enforced by emperors. This peace could become reality when people chose to be redeemed in Christ.

Simeon recognized God's plan to allow him, a servant, to "depart in peace" (Luke 2:29). As a master released a slave from keeping watch, so God released Simeon to die. His work was done. The Prince of Peace had come.

Later, Jesus sent messengers to tell others about a new way of living. They were to say, "Peace be to this house" (Luke 10:5). The customary oriental greeting—said when meeting or leaving another—

was "Peace be to you." Jesus added a choice. Hearers could either accept or reject salvation through the Redeemer. If they refused the blessing, it would be returned to those who gave it.

The term peace also occurs in praise to God during Jesus' triumphal entry into Jerusalem. "Blessed be the King who comes in the name of the Lord! Peace in heaven and glory in the highest!" (Luke 19:38). This recalls the chorus of angels at Jesus' birth (Luke 2:14). It affirms that God deserves praise for preparing peace in heaven. In coming to humanity, Jesus established true peace between humanity and divinity. Hosanna! resounds.

But disappointment and surprise awaited the Palm Sunday crowd. When the resurrected Christ said, "Peace be with you" (John 20:19, 21, 26), he was expressing more than a greeting. Those who felt forsaken or were startled heard again the promise given during the Last Supper: "Peace I leave with you; my peace I give to you." Christ's gift of peace to the disciples was to accompany them as peacemakers.

Most Epistles (except Hebrews, James, and 1 John) begin and end with some expression of granting peace (Rom. 15:33, 16:20; 1 Cor. 16:11; 2 Cor. 13:11; Gal. 6:16; Eph. 6:23; Phil. 4:7, 9; 1 Thess. 5:23). "Peace be with you," so commonly used among Jewish people, may have had little meaning. But when connected with grace, mercy, or love as a gift of God, it stressed the conviction that as "Peace" or Savior, Christ brings wholeness.

On four occasions Luke ends an encounter with

Jesus by joining faith, salvation, and peace (well-being). To the grateful woman who anointed his feet (7:50), Jesus said, "Your faith has saved you; go in peace."

He gave the blessing to the woman freed of a strange flow of blood, "Daughter, your faith has made you well; go in peace" (8:48).

He told the blind beggar (18:42) and the one grateful man relieved of leprosy, "Rise and go your way; your faith has made you well" (17:19).

Because of faith, people were forgiven. They knew inner wholeness. Because of faith, people knew healing. Because of faith, they went in peace —saved. As belief made them grateful, people were fully cured. They then chose to follow this Friend rather than other power figures.

Peace and Racial Discord

Numerous texts show the complexity of achieving peace. We experience that too. What we justify determines our actions. We may carry resentment. We may deny our own bias. We may let lack of knowledge shape opinion. Or we may sincerely work to counter these, but never fully succeed. The same was true of biblical conflict.

Several stories about Samaritans show the complexity of achieving peace. Jesus showed his Jewish listeners that precisely those people they justified excluding were to be welcomed in God's new ordering of life. Here's why this racial conflict existed.

During Israel's life under the kings, the Samaritan people hoped for a prophet, or restorer, like Moses. They looked for a deliverer, Taheb, while later Israelites longed for an anointed king, like David.

When the Northern Kingdom (Israel) fell to Assyrian rule, most people were deported. Those who remained married immigrants moving into the region. The Jews of the Southern Kingdom (Judah) thought that those mixed people living in Israel, later known as Samaritans, were impure.

When the Jews from Judah returned from exile in Babylon, they refused to let the Samaritans help rebuild the Jerusalem Temple. So the Samaritans did their best to hinder the work. Sharp conflict, including many deaths, followed.

Although Jewish law forbade having a temple outside Jerusalem, the Samaritans built their own on Mount Gerizim. They also formed their own rival priesthood.

Major crises followed. Hyrcanus, a Jewish Hasmomean ruler, destroyed the Gerizim temple and the city of Samaria more than a century before Jesus' time. During Jesus' childhood, the Samaritans defiled the Jerusalem Temple by placing bones in the sanctuary during a Passover festival. Several decades after Jesus' death the feud stirred mass murders and revenge killings.

This discontent can be seen in the account in *Luke 9:51-56*. Jesus and his circle of followers were on their way to Jerusalem through Samaria. Aware of conflicts between pilgrims and local residents, Jesus' group asked for lodging and meals in a village. The Samaritans refused. Perhaps they would not help anyone headed for worship at the hated Temple. Perhaps they knew Jesus' group would not honor Mount Gerizim as they passed through Samaria.

Hearing the messengers' report, James and John asked Jesus if he, like Elijah, might send down fire to consume those who refused hospitality. But compassion could not condone revenge. Jesus encouraged his followers to tolerate rather than violently oppose enemies. He restated the principle of nonresistance to evil. Choosing to be fully human, to embody the image of God in which humanity had been originally created, Jesus had come to save and not to destroy people.

Such new lessons about social order were difficult to learn. Resentment and retaliation only deepened the conflict. Limits to well-being for all died slowly.

Another incident, perhaps the most familiar, features the good Samaritan (*Luke 10:25-37*). How difficult for a Jew to put those two words together —to have *good* describe a Samaritan.

To help us understand, we need to put "good" before whatever group or individual we resent or exclude—Russians, people with same sex preference or a disease like AIDS, or those who do not let us control them.

To what extent do we name these our neighbor? Would we give mercy to or receive it from them? Or might we also make excuses? We do not want to defile ourselves or mar our reputation. Or perhaps we try but find the stance too lonely.

Luke had a special interest in Samaritans, those considered *outside* by the orthodox *insiders*. Who could be more orthodox than a Jewish lawyer to care for the 613 rules used to justify one's actions?

What a deep challenge to legalism was thus inherent in Jesus' answer to a lawyer's question about eternal life. First Jesus reshaped concern for salvation by works. He told the lawyer, who knew the two basic commandments, just *do* them! Stop using your rules to excuse inaction!

The lawyer then asked the critical question, "Who is my neighbor?" The answer buried in the story Jesus then told, of a *Samaritan* who modeled love for neighbor, must have thoroughly unnerved the lawyer.

Those who heard about the man who was robbed and beaten on the barren road between Jerusalem and Jericho were informed. They knew that many priests and Levites returned home to Jericho when off duty at the Temple. They knew about the thieves or bandits who hid in the region. They knew that businessmen of Samaria traveled there and that many travelers carried healing agents, such as oil and wine.

Hearers might at least have expected the caregiver to be a Jew without religious title. The issue then would have been discontent with Jewish hierarchy.

Instead, help comes from a member of a despised people. And this compassionate Samaritan not only offers first aid but goes out of his way to meet all the man's needs. He even offers to pay for additional costs on his return. To hear a hated Samaritan commended for model behavior, or that Jews could be helped by Samaritans, forced hearers to deal with their racial hatred and conflict.

If we think only people like us are neighbors, we can exclude others. If we feel responsible only for those who support our views, who drink tea the way we do, or with whom we exchange favors, our concept of neighbor is narrow.

The Peacemaker, who was both priest and prophet, called for new depth of understanding. Forcing the lawyer to stop hiding behind technicalities, he turned the lawyer's verbal skill into a call for him to *be* neighbor to others.

And Jesus refused to allow a narrow definition of neighbor that would let the lawyer and other orthodox insiders "off the hook." *Any* person in need was a neighbor. Eternal life comes to those who provide well-being to all, beginning with those pushed to the society's edges.

Luke was persistent. He wanted readers to comprehend Jesus' radical message: both Jews *and* non-Jews were to join in God's just ordering of life. If we exclude some people, we counter peace and fail to demonstrate the nature of God's kingdom.

Another model Samaritan appears in *Luke 17:11-19.* Near the border between Samaria and Galilee, Jesus met ten people who had leprosy. They cried for mercy. One of those considered ritually unclean was Samaritan; the others were Jews.

Delaying a miracle, the Healer told them to go to

their respective priests. As they went, in faith that the cure would happen, they experienced it. The skin disease that had made them outcasts disappeared.

All could have decided to wait for the priest to pronounce them "clean" before expressing thanks. But one, the Samaritan, returned first to thank the Healer. Only one chose to glorify God first. While all were healed, the Samaritan modeled response to receiving well-being or salvation. Responsive faith, not race, led to peace.

Peace and Family Discord

Biblical stories also reveal discord in families. *Luke 10:38-42* records Jesus' visit to the home of Martha and Mary in Bethany. Here are two sisters and their close Friend. Here is conflict over roles, over being and doing.

Perhaps a widow and the owner of the home, Martha seems upset. Her duty was to offer hospitality. Yet she no doubt wanted to join Mary who listened to and interacted with the Teacher. Demonstrating a healthy sense of self, Martha confronted Jesus. No doubt Mary often helped with domestic work. But when given the opportunity to learn the Torah, she put household duty second.

Jesus' practice of including women when he taught religious truth itself caused conflict. Women were excluded from learning the Torah. Jesus attacked that injustice. He enabled women to be informed witnesses. He showed that peace or well-being is possible for all only when experience is more mutual.

Even as Martha felt her service was unappreciated, Jesus stated that Mary had wisely chosen to learn discipleship. From John's story of the death of Lazarus (11:27), we learn that Martha also knew about discipleship. Confident, she confessed: "Yes, Lord; I believe that you are the Christ, the Son of God, he who is coming into the world."

But Luke's story of her pain at being saddled with the chores surfaced. So she and Jesus spoke frankly. He gently chided her excess concern to provide for him, even though her work also proved her love.

Service to others can be distracting if not balanced with personal growth and devotion to God. Overdoing or neglecting either contemplation or action helps neither. Martha's anxiety about duty led her to understand that giving less time to some tasks can release time for developing faith.

Concern for fairness in families is also valid. Roles deserve to be duly shared. And feelings need to be expressed. Not to confront injustice shows as much lack of peace or well-being as addressing it may cause. Mary did not quit learning with her Teacher. And freed from a sense of excess duty, Martha grew as a disciple.

Another New Testament text referring to peace is *Luke 12:51-53:* "Do you think that I have come to give peace on earth? No, I tell you, but rather division. . . ." Some Christians have a false concept of peace. Absence of conflict is their main concern. When these judge other believers involved in conflict, they extend conflict. At times, well-being emerges only through conflict. This may follow when justice is denied, when one party refuses to repent, or when people choose to deprive others of social or economic stature.

Jews expected the coming Messiah to bring Jewish victory over every enemy or nation. But victory that fails to give advantage to everyone involved is always partial. The desire to dominate, which is the essence of sin, fails to understand God's radically different order (kingdom). A later chapter develops this theme.

Jesus knew he would bring dissension. As he confronted established religious and social patterns, conflict would develop. Family members and generations would differ. Enmity would follow. Many who joined this Dissenter would be hated or persecuted. Yet he always pointed ahead to God's coming as complete peace.

Jesus invited people to true discipleship in spite of the cost (*Luke 14:26-27*). His teaching to hate father and mother may sound harsh. In Semitic thought the word often translated *hate* means to *love less*. God's devoted disciples avoid being possessive about family. They ask, "Who are my mother and brother?" All who do the will of God claim the Redeemer. When conflict over following Christ causes broken bonds, believers will continue to love family members—even though they appear to love them less.

Peace and Religious Discord

Religious authorities could not tolerate Jesus'

acts of healing on the Sabbath (*Luke 6:6-11; 13:10-17; 14:1-6*). Since scribes and Pharisees watched to find fault, Jesus acted openly. Standing by the man whose hand was withered, he asked the leaders about doing good on the Sabbath. Is refusal to save life similar to destroying it?

The sensible question irritated them. Jesus' ability to know the thoughts and desires of others added to the discord. His power to restore a part of the body through words could not be denied. To point out the obvious was disturbing. Who among the crowd did not, on some Sabbath, have an animal fall into a pit or well? When this happened, did they work to get it out of agony? Or who among them did not untie their animal and lead it to water on the Sabbath?

By comparison, would Jesus be wrong to help a person out of misery? The point was doubly sharp since they considered the woman Jesus healed to be property, like an animal.

Nothing in Scripture forbade healing. Yet rabbis created new rules when interpreting the law. For example, they said that only in extreme cases could healing be done on the Sabbath. It was work. A woman whose spine was deformed for eighteen years could not be seen as facing an emergency. Jesus attacked this valuing of ritual laws over people in need. Human life must be valued.

Although Jesus broke some ritual laws, he never broke the Sabbath. He rested and worshiped God regularly in the Temple. He destroyed Satan's control of peoples' lives on that day. He confronted leaders with the weakness of their rationale for killing him. How could murder be valid Sabbath activity? Too often, those most guilty of breaking the sacred Sabbath are hypocritical and proud of their own "holiness."

Another occasion of discord was the Temple cleanup (*Luke 19:45-46*). While John records this as Jesus' first great public act of ministry, other writers place it during Jesus' last week. The Challenger would not allow the Temple to be used as a commercial bazaar. To exchange coins for travelers or sell ritually clean animals for sacrifice was all right. But the Court of the Gentiles was being profaned. Not only had it become a city shortcut. It also hosted corruption, greed, and racial prejudice.

A Messiah was expected to bring reform. Direct conflict with those guarding religious power was inevitable. When Jesus stopped their profit making, their scorn increased. The Reformer expressed disfavor through the neutral emotion of anger. Priest and prophet merged. Truly to image God involves both kindness and severity (Rom. 11:22).

Jesus denounced evil and evildoers. The high priest family of Annas had become rich at the expense of others. Jesus therefore restored a place for the deprived Gentiles, so that they could pray to God. In this event Jesus revealed God as surely as he did on the cross. Wrath is part of holiness. Discord that results from confronting injustice and insisting on well-being is part of peacemaking

We find far less war imagery in the New Testament than in the Old. Yet there are references to swords, either real or as metaphor (*Luke 22:35-38, 49-53*). If read literally, the first section is confusing. Then Jesus urges violence which contradicts his clear commitment to peace.

Seen as metaphor, the Teacher warns the disciples to prepare for the future. Isaiah 53:12 must be fulfilled. Jesus will become one with—or take the place of—sinners. Rejected, he will not be with believers much longer. They will need to find their way within a hostile world. Therefore, he urges, be courageous, be determined, be like an armed fighter who continues to struggle.

Speaking in metaphor, Jesus tells the disciples to know what armor of the Spirit is theirs. But they miss the point. Someone says, "Lord, we have two swords."

To this a frustrated Jesus sadly replies, "Enough of this! Say no more." Their failure to understand may destroy him.

Luke then tells about the motley, armed crowd that came to arrest Jesus on the Mount of Olives. Not yet comprehending his refusal to meet violence with violence, the disciples wonder if they should use force to prevent the arrest. In fact, impulsive Peter cuts an ear off Malchus, the slave of the high priest. Peter fails to realize this could make Jesus appear to be a leader of violent people. Jesus reminded the disciples that God's way is not the world's violent way. They watched as the Peacemaker gave himself to God's purpose and plan.

According to those who wished Pilate to get rid

of him, Jesus was anything but a peacemaker (*Luke 23:1-5, 13-25*). He was called disturber of the peace. Threat to public order. Perverter of people and nation. He encouraged people to give first place to God, not Caesar. He claimed to be king.

To get rid of the troublemaker, groups who normally hated each other joined efforts. They opposed his call for a new social pattern which refused privilege to the mighty and granted new dignity and opportunity to those limited by society.

Their charges of self-appointed kingship were unfair. Not understanding a servant stance that empowers, they thought of kingship as embodying control and domination. But Jesus' style of order and peace was not what the Jews expected from a Messiah. Nor was it what Roman officials modeled.

Yet Pilate tried to dismiss the case, offering to reprimand the defendant. He saw the peoples' malice. This was no criminal. So the religious authorities whipped up the masses to pressure Pilate. The approach could not have been less just for a Prince of Peace offering well-being to all.

Jesus had warned believers to expect persecution (*Luke 21:10-19*). He had also assured them of God's presence. Through them, God would address opponents. In the radical cause of Jesus, few would escape hatred, betrayal, or death. But to endure to the end is the call.

John's gospel agrees. Jesus invites believers into conflict with the world (John 15:18-20). Followers can expect trouble since Jesus said what people resented. He endorsed a new order, reshaped *peace*.

A Final Example

To conclude the focus on peace or well-being,
imagine that you are reading *Ahebwa's Journal Ex-
cerpts*. She is from Uganda. Recall the woman
known for her hemorrhage (*Luke 8:43-48*).

■ ■ ■

APRIL 20. Who will listen? I'm just Ahebwa, the
woman with the strange disease. What have I
done to deserve this long agony? Why was I
born? For what good did I marry? Who could expect him to stay with me, in my condition? All
the tears that have flowed into my cot over this
wretched flow of blood could create a pool. I
simply can't endure much longer like this—
drained.

MAY 11. Blood. Red blood. Shades of redness.
Blood—the stuff of life. But for me, death in life.
Every day, as present as breath. Why not one or
the other? I wonder . . . what's worse than disease? An unclean body makes it useless. Ahebwa
—sociable but always held at arms length. Willing to work in the fields, but farmers won't let
me harvest the groundnuts or millet or sweet po-
tatoes. My blood defiles soil.

JUNE 8. I used to think this would quit. Dreams
break into long nights, chasing the stars and with
them my pain. Then I wake up and know—nothing has changed. How long? Who knows? Time
matters not for Ahebwa. Day follows night. Dusk
precedes dawn. I hardly know which leads into

the other. Twelve years of days and twelve years of nights.

After one dream, I thought the right doctor had come. The medicine woman prescribed a new mixture. No need to chant with this one. The traditional herbs seem to have lost their power with Ahebwa. Each time I muster the energy to contact a more distant medicine woman, I'm disappointed. And shamed . . . for thinking a cure might be found.

JUNE 18. Last evening, when walking near the village's main tree, I paused in the shadows and listened to the men. Word traveled about a man known to heal. A mixture of compassion and harsh expectation. As the men sipped their *chai* (milk tea), little did they realize how I, Ahebwa, longed to meet that Healer. I'll eavesdrop again . . . then weigh the risks of asking my neighbor —the one neighbor who doesn't ignore me—for more details. This Healer may be no more than another dream.

JULY 2. How I long to go to the place of worship! But people know about Ahebwa. I don't want to defile the sacred, but I can hardly remember the different rituals and the cowry shells. The chickens offered on my behalf would make a flock! But God appears not to have heard their dying clucks. At least no healing has come. That a flicker of hope remains kindled in my breasts is a miracle. Must be a Divine spark.

JULY 13. I'm unclean. Unworthy. Why should I expect anyone to greet me on the path? I walk when others will not be around. Stares used to hurt. Children's conversations—based on what they hear from adults—no longer intrude on my thoughts. How I enjoyed the nieces and nephews who bounced on my lap. But now they disperse, their faces glancing sideways in fear. Just what is friendship for Ahebwa?

JULY 29. (Early morning) What's the noise? Half the village moves by my hut, carrying lanterns. They chatter excitedly. Maybe if I put my cot in front of the doorway, I'll hear more. . . . The Healer! Yes. That's what they said. They're going to see him. Rather than lying here thinking it's useless, I'm going. Even if I only touch his garment—a corner of his outer cloth—some power may come to me.

(Midday) I stop to eat bananas and groundnut sauce. What an odd feeling I have—like inner peace. Fear has evaporated with the rising sun. A desire to just get close to the Healer spurs me on. Oh, they're moving again. From the sounds, he must be just around the bend, near the next village.

(A little later) What a crowd! I haven't been this close to people for years. At least my own village people won't notice me. Now, I'm not going to delay the Healer—just touch him in passing. But I do think this will make a difference. I'm going to be well again. Imagine!

Oh, that must be he. The child next to him seems sick. I won't slow him down. But I must get closer. Thank goodness, he doesn't notice me.

But people do make getting next to him hard.
There, if I slip between those two. . . . This will
make me whole again. There, I did it!

God of Israel! What relief. My hemorrhage
quit. Just like that. Am I losing my mind too?
What a moment! Let me get out of here and hide
until I get myself pulled together.

What's that? The Healer insists that everyone
stop. Who touched him? Those next to him laugh.
His question is absurd, with so many people
around.

But I touched him. And I knew his power. I'm
no longer the same Ahebwa. Can he tell that? If
so, there's probably no choice but to confess.
He's asking, again.

I only meant to touch. But he wants this to be
more public. Healer, I come with trust, yet fear,
deep inside. With gratitude, I'll tell my story. . . .

"Go in peace." That's what he concluded. With
affection, he called me his daughter. Even when
he knew about my blood, he didn't think he had
been defiled. He denounces legal details that
separate.

He credited my faith. Imagine, Ahebwa's faith!
He gave me the blessing, "Be free from your af-
fliction." Oh, to be free, to go in peace. To be
whole and worthy again. What a day!

How can I let others know about the Healer?
Perhaps I'll share my journal. Perhaps Ahebwa's
story will let others know about true *peace*.

CHAPTER 2

Justice, or Being Empowered

Many people today talk about justice. While some hesitate to disrupt "things as they are," others work vigorously for equity despite the barriers posed by tradition. Christians find a basis for justice-making in their understanding of God: To know God is to do justice (Jeremiah 22:16).

To know God is not merely to worship God or comply with certain doctrine. Nor is it most enhanced by pious phrases. To act on behalf of the mistreated indicates that one knows God. "Conversely," as Robert McAfee Brown notes, "the sign of not knowing God is to do injustice."[4]

True peace or well-being is impossible without justice. Injustice in family, church, and state systems must be confronted. Jesus set the example. Besides aiding the needy, justice-making addresses discrimination. It questions rigid structures that defy change and relationships that destroy.

Christianity is not biblical when it ignores God's wish for salvation, justice, and empowerment for all. Salvation is often defined as individual peace with God. But it means more, including wholeness within (a healthy self-esteem) and right relationship with God and neighbor. As Dorothee Soelle says, "Christian faith cannot be understood outside involvement in liberation struggles."[5]

During recent decades, Latin American liberation theology has called Christians worldwide to see the Bible's first priority as justice for the poor. Asian and African theologians are also shaping understandings of God suitable for their cultures.

These efforts show how inadequate western (European and North American) theology has been. According to Gustavo Gutierrez, the first question is not how to talk about God in our world. Rather, it is, "How are we to tell people who are scarcely human that God is love and that God's love makes us one family?"[6]

Duty toward God is not based, says Brown, on "Do you know the creed? Do you pray? Are you careful about Sabbath observance? Do you mention God in your constitution and on your coins?" It's based on "What did you do for those in need?"[7] New awareness of God's judgment of nations, groups, and individuals who oppress offers hope.

The goal is to replace an imbalance of power and resources with mutual control that empowers all. God calls both oppressors and oppressed to change. For the same person may sometimes be an oppressor and at other times oppressed.

Oppression takes many shapes. There cruel political and economic structures. There are rich and powerful people who gain wealth at the expense of others.

Other theologians describe Christian oppression in a variety of ways. Using only masculine terms or images for the divine. Blessing dualism or divisions that devalue the body or history. Defining power or the order of creation in hierarchical (top to bottom) ways. Thinking of divine power as imperial. Believing that only Christians know truth. Defining sin as pride and rebellion but not as determination to dominate.[8]

Many believe that *Luke 4:16-30* was the inaugural address of Jesus' ministry. A homily presented in his hometown of Nazareth, it summarizes his mission. As the Messiah, he will release victims. He will restore people to wholeness. He will transform societies. These visionary goals were not, however, fully achieved before his death.

Jesus calls us who claim to follow him to continue his mission. We are to bring good news to the poor. We are to proclaim liberty to all captives, release to the imprisoned, God's blessing on the oppressed. We are to release, restore, and transform. To be a disciple means to confront injustice and minister to the oppressed. As Jesus probed the root causes of problems, so will believers. Through transforming society we show compassion.

Those who work for justice will be loved by some and hated by others. People deprived of power, opportunity, or the basics of survival will be grateful for efforts on their behalf. People asked to more truly share wealth, control, or privilege may resent and then misrepresent the cause of justice. This may be done either directly or subtly.

Current Efforts to Empower

Examples of work for justice are numerous. During military rule in Uruguay, more citizens were made political prisoners and cruelly tortured. When peace and justice advocates protested this lack of human rights, authorities destroyed their organization. They protected their system from change. They deprived people of a voice. Fear, not strength, impelled them. Fear of another's strength compared to one's own underlies dominance.

Questions of language about God and people are questions of justice or empowering. God is Spirit and Action and Being, not male or female. So to avoid idolatry and do justice to God's diversity, the words that describe God need to be multiple and varied, not restricted.

Language about people also needs to make clear who is meant. Both women and men deserve to be distinctly named. To include women in male terms minimizes women. It suggests that maleness is normative while femaleness is "other." This in turn fosters the sin of male domination.

As demands for dowry in India increase, giving birth to daughters causes increased fear. Each family knows that the cost of getting a daughter married will be great. It drives many into severe debt. Once married, the husband or in-laws often pressure the young wife for more money than originally specified. She has little recourse to justice. The number of young bride deaths, explained as "accidental," is alarming. Some women leaders are confronting Christians who marry with dowry.

Too often we accuse the homeless of poor management. We ignore the multiple factors causing their state, such as unjust federal budget priorities. Thus we avoid our need to change. This approves, rather than confronts, the status quo.

The prime tasks are to help victims directly and to confront oppressive systems that permit indulgence for some and scarcity for others. Christians prone to consume resources often minimize the effect of their wealth on those with inadequate food, shelter, health care, or dignity.

The politics of dominance support the status quo. Economic, social, or cultural systems that withhold benefits from those who deserve them do violence. A patriarchal society assigns secondary status to woman. It assigns lower value to their economic, social, religious, or political roles. Being considered objects lowers women's self-esteem. They become more vulnerable to rape, pornography, and poverty. They need to be empowered.

Prophetic Calls for Justice

In his inaugural address, Jesus claims he is beginning to fulfill the prediction of *Isaiah 61*. Empowered by Yahweh's spirit, the prophet had begun the Jubilee year preaching God's good news. The news was good for some—the poor without privilege, those broken or desperate because of judgments against them, those patiently awaiting the Messiah.

Although no longer in exile, the Israelites remained oppressed by the Romans and their own corrupt rulers. To them the prophet announces liberty. God is coming to their rescue. Their keeper wants them to rejoice—through festive events, garlands, and oils—rather than to mourn.

God calls Israel to become sturdy oaks of justice, rebuilding what was long in ruins. For God loves justice, hates crime, and wants to reward Israel through a covenant that blesses them into the future. Given new moral fiber, the people determine to grow as a garden planted by the Gardener.

Such is the background for Jesus' mission in Luke. But whereas the Isaiah message was welcomed, Jesus' hearers were first glad—then wished his death. Isaiah's good news meant that Israel would conquer its foes. But Jesus rejects a violent, nationalistic triumph. He rebukes the racial and religious pride of the people of the synagogue. Despised Gentiles, such as widows and those with leprosy, will hear and be healed by God's Word. But many of the synagogue will reject it.[9]

The good news will anger those who oppose empowering the disadvantaged. It will cause those committed to justice, like Jesus, to be prophetic. But who is a prophet? Jewish professor Abraham Heschel suggests that to be a prophet means to identify one's concern with the concern of God. "A sense of care for God's care is the personal prerequisite for being a prophet."[10] To "know thy God" leads to being prophetic.

Prophets listen carefully to God's concerns. They

believe that God's care is for all. And their efforts
are to empower all. They never imply that salvation
is only an individual matter. Not endowed with
unique knowledge, true prophets receive truth consistent with earlier prophets. The writers of Isaiah
had enduring concerns. Mary's song in *Luke 1:46-
55* repeated what Hannah had said years before.

As the first Christian disciple, Mary spoke for the
Poor Ones, a remnant of Israelites. Decades have
come and gone since Jesus' mother stated her con-
viction. Current conditions still fail to fully reflect
God's concern. But partial truth came recently to
Eskimo and Indian people of the Pacific Northwest.
Nine major church groups apologized for arrogant
Christian destruction of the spiritual practices and
sacred rites of Native peoples.[11]

As Robert McAfee Brown reports from Latin
America, "There are few biblical passages more
widely used than Mary's song."[12] Oppressed people
yearn for the reversal she predicted. They wait for
more of us to choose to share wealth, power, and
position—to overcome pride.

Brown tells about the end of a worship service in
Lima, Peru. Thousands had gathered to ponder how
theology, Scripture, and spirituality could help
overcome poverty and injustice in their villages.
Leaving the meeting, they started to sing Mary's
song.[13]

> Those who had every reason to wonder whether
> God could even be called a God of justice and
> power were singing, "God has shown strength with

God's arm. . . ." Those who had been threatened and imprisoned by leaders whose grip on power seemed secure were singing, "God has put down the mighty from their thrones. . . ." Those who worried about food for themselves and their children were singing, "God has filled the hungry with good things."

Mary's *Magnificat* is indeed a prelude to Jesus' message. She reassures those condemned and scorned. She combines politics with religion. She knows God's care will turn things upside down.

While the lowly are lifted up, those who manipulate are cast down. While the insecure gain a new sense of self, the proud are scattered, never to put it all together again. While the "have nots" take matters into their own hands, the "haves" balk and stew at this threat. Truly Mary's is a song of thanks for God's liberating acts. It is a call to revolutionary following.

Those who manipulate, are proud, or have an unfair share of anything, will choose their response to this message. They may countercharge, saying that those who do not endorse their position are unjust. They may argue that anyone who works for it can share their wealth, power, or privilege.

Or they may change. They may find that to control less, to be less arrogant, or to share advantage offers more personal freedom. They may therefore open themselves to the principles involved and gradually take simple but profound steps to gain release from their addiction to control.

Justice and Possessions

There are several sections on justice in *Luke 12*. Verses 13-15 tell of a man from the crowd who asked Jesus to help him get his part of an inheritance. He expected Jesus to intervene, but Jesus refused. His role was not to arbitrate family disputes about possessions. His vision of both family and ownership were broader. Those who listen to and act according to the divine Parent's word are family to each other.

Feuds about what belongs to whom imply greed. Complaints about inheritance (money, possessions, honor, prestige, or power) are petty when some people have nothing to inherit.

This is followed by a parable about a rich man faced with a surplus harvest (*12:16-21*). He looked out first for himself. He tore down his small warehouses and built bigger barns with little thought of others and their need.

Looking ahead to carefree retirement, he pretended that death could not alter his future. But God saw the fool. His plans to enlarge his stockpile ignored God's concern for justice. His death that night verified the folly of hoarding wealth while neglecting others. It exposed the rich fool's poverty.

Luke includes other stories that contrast the rich and poor, that emphasize justice in economic and social matters. Recall the woe to those who already have their reward (6:24). The rich one's pleading with Lazarus from Hades (16:19-26). The approach of the Good Samaritan (10:35-7). The invitation list

for the feast (14:13). The reversal of Zacchaeus
(19:2-9). The prudence of the dishonest steward
(16:1-9). And the contrast in Acts of a spirit of
community sharing (2:42-47; 4:32-35) with the de-
ception of Ananias and Sapphira (5:1-11).

Jesus had good counsel for a host about to invite
people to a party or dinner (*Luke 14:12-14*). Instead of inviting only those who can return the favor, think of the needy who can never repay. Give
them an occasion to enjoy. Remember Israel's story
of being sojourners without power or influence.
Avoid judging people as marginal or unworthy of
honor. Such principles endure for any guest list.

On hearing this counsel, another said, "Blessed
are those who get to enjoy or eat bread in God's
kingdom." Again Jesus had a story about fair opportunity (*14:15-24*). When guests invited to a great
banquet made excuses, the householder sent his
servant into the city's lanes and streets. Any who
chose to look out for a new field or oxen or new
spouse could be ignored. Even when some turned
down the offer, the banquet continued.

Those whose handicaps or poverty caused their
exclusion were welcomed. Cautious, yet delighted,
they noticed other outcasts. They sensed how the
"haves" who were present welcomed them. With
the dining hall still not full, the servant went out
again, to the highways and byways beyond the town
(to include the Gentiles). Those who first rejected
the offer were replaced.

Matters of justice here are clear. People presum-
ing to have privilege have much to learn. The ta-

bles will be turned. When the "favored" reject God's will, others are soon invited. In the process, a new order that opposes classes of people is created. All who enter God's kingdom are invited and empowered. Those not seated have chosen not to be there. That's fair.

In another incident of reversal (*Luke 16:19-31*), a rich man and a Lazarus (not Martha and Mary's brother) are key characters. Two themes occur. (1) Expect fortunes to be reversed in the next life. (2) If the law and the prophets fail to bring the rich to repentance, one raised from the dead cannot do it.

Perhaps Jesus borrowed details of this parable from Egyptian and then Jewish folk lore. Perhaps he was warning that no further sign would be given to those who refused to hear the Word of God. The message of justice, plus gentle hints for avoiding the dilemma, are embedded in the story.

Contrasts are clear. The rich man had purple or costly garments, even fine underwear. Lazarus was covered with sores. Dogs licking the ulcers offered little relief. The rich man ate splendidly while Lazarus went hungry.

But the rich man and his friends did nothing to help the ill or crippled beggar outside the gate. After death, how tormented the rich man was. How comfortably Lazarus rested in Abraham's bosom.

Not aware of their reversed positions, the rich man thought he could still control. He asked Abraham to send Lazarus with water to quench his thirst caused by intense heat. But the gulf between could not be crossed.

The rich man made a final command: Send Lazarus with a message to my brothers. Tell them that to ignore the poor will bring them doom. And what was the response? Let your family pay attention to human rights and the prophets. Let justice—which is worship in action—shape their destiny.

Leaders: Will They Oppress or Empower?

Luke 9:28-43 includes a call to integrate social action with reflection. The occasion was Jesus' transfiguration when response to human need directly followed worship. The place of revelation was probably Mt. Meron, just northwest of the Sea of Galilee. Recall the details. A supernatural change in Jesus' face and clothing. The cloud—or presence and voice of God. The presence of Moses the liberator and Elijah the prophet, who defended the oppressed.

Peter wished to prolong the experience. He wanted to withdraw into "the spiritual," to revel in mystery, to build a retreat center. He wanted to build three booths—to stay and enjoy. He wanted shelters—even leafy, short-term structures like those built at the Feast of Tabernacles or harvest.

But true worship stirs concern for human need. It serves more than the worshiper. Jesus returned from the mountain and proceeded to heal a fellow tormented by something like epilepsy. This is the cycle: social action expresses the spiritual, and worship grows out of action on behalf of the oppressed, for it gives praise to God.

Too few religious leaders of Jesus' day connected

faith and justice. (See *Luke 20:45—21:4*, written when Christians faced persecution.) Hostility between church and synagogue was growing. Jesus charged the interpreters of the law with practicing piety while oppressing widows. Long prayers and keen verbal tactics were not the solution.

Their love of public honor through exalted status or distinct religious dress and address was the problem. The pious would not repent from this worship of false gods. Their obedience to the law blessed a dead formalism.

Although scribes were expected to provide teaching without fees, some exploited widows by encouraging them to give gifts in exchange. Defenseless as widows were, they gave more than they could afford if they were poor or than was proper if they were rich. When Jesus confronted this exploitation, he stirred scribal wrath.

Who could more honestly illustrate the Teacher's point than a poor widow? The rich brought their gifts to the trumpet-shaped chests in the treasury room. A widow brought her two copper coins. Jewish law did not permit giving less than two of this smallest coin in circulation. Each giver told the priest the amount and purpose for an offering.

Whereas the rich gave out of their surplus, this widow gave all she had, which was earmarked for her next meal. Hers was a gift of faith. Giving out of surplus is hardly noticed. Giving by the wealthy to compensate for their social injustices is hardly more noble. Among the "poorest of the poor," with few ways to earn, this widow was most generous.

An earlier text (*Luke 11:42-44*) faults a related gesture, the Pharisaic practice of tithing everything but neglecting justice. The tithe law—found in Leviticus 27:30 and Deuteronomy 14:22—states, "You shall tithe all the yield of your seed, which comes forth from the field year by year."

In Jesus' day, even kitchen herbs and flowers were to be tithed. This unfairly burdened poor people. Whereas tithing should express a joyful offering of love, religious legalism stressed trivia and caused class distinctions. In the process, true piety and justice were neglected.

Unwilling to admit varied sins of injustice, the Pharisees needed externals with which to comply. But Jesus wished them to consecrate themselves and their possessions to God—to empower others because of their love for God. Too often their zealous motivation focused on the self. For example, they loved to be in the public eye and to have others defer to them. They wished for the best seat in the synagogue—the semicircular bench in front of the ark, facing the congregation.

Jesus' "woe" was sharp. Pharisees, he said, were like unseen graves that made a person who walked over them unclean. Hiding their true nature, they corrupted others or led those who imitated them to become hypocrites. Their pride and biases were dangerous because they promoted injustice.

Another text (*Luke 18:9-14*) describes the faithful. Prayers of a Pharisee and a tax collector are overheard in the Temple. The former recites how pious he is. Twice a week he fasts (a practice of

GOSHEN COLLEGE LIBRARY
GOSHEN, INDIANA

zealous Jews). He tithes his entire income, not just certain crops or farm products. With contempt, he judges and condemns others. He feels indifferent toward the wretched.

By contrast, a hated tax collector considers himself a sinner. Unworthy before God, he is unworthy of friendship with others. Aware of his guilt, he faults himself. Not lifting his eyes (the usual practice), and beating his breast, he begs God for mercy.

In order to understand Jesus' teaching, we need to know how much tax collectors were despised. Their task was unpleasant—to collect land, poll, and indirect taxes on purchases or goods in transit, plus customs. Many did abuse people who failed to pay the sometimes heavy dues. Even if collectors repented, they were not always accepted, because restitution was hard to achieve.

A parable in which a tax collector, rather than a religious leader, modeled true repentance confounded the hearers. Unable to imagine or accept a story in which a collector of tolls was faithful, they misunderstood both God's kingdom and discipleship. Yet Jesus approved an attitude of faith and humility toward God, rather than a record of piety and legalism.

Verse 14b echoes the theme of reversal to come. The proud will be brought down and the lowly raised. If not always now, justice will be realized in the future.

A Final Example

To conclude this section on empowering through justice, hear Maria's persistent tale from Brazil. This is a dialogue based on Jesus' parable about a widow and an unjust judge (*Luke 18:2-5*).

■ ■ ■

Maria Carolina: I understand you are the judge for this *pueblito* (village). I am a widow; my husband died four months ago. Now that the time has come for planting, I have the double burden of caring for my family and raising enough grain to sell a little.

Judge: How often I hear the same tale.

Maria: Further, my brother-in-law took my machete and hoe. Says he has a right to what was his dead brother's. With his son old enough to help farm, tools are needed for him. While I was at the *feria* (market) last Thursday, the brother came and took them. My child noticed but knew he couldn't question his elder. . . .

Judge: I'm really not interested in all this detail.

Maria: I took the brother's family *una flauta de pan* (a loaf of bread) yesterday and asked for my machete and hoe. Taking the bread without thanks, the brother said that what they have is their's. His wife, stirring food at the little stove, never turned to notice me. I left, dismayed.

Judge: That's life, isn't it?

Maria: Now I've come to you, since you are a judge with the task of calling for justice.

Judge: I can't make it happen by myself.

Maria: I know. You'll need to get this brother to co-operate.

Judge: Only after you try harder. Go back to him. He must be good at heart. Go on!

(Four days later)

Maria: Judge, my brother refuses. Says the machete and hoe are his . . . that they're busy getting their fields ready.

Judge: So, get them back when he's finished planting.

Maria: But I need your help now. Have you been a widow? I mean, have you ever heard cases of widows?

Judge: Ever? Widows often complain! Never generous either.

Maria: Oh, judge. Are you wishing for a bribe? I simply can't bargain with you. I haven't money to buy my child the medicine she needs. I can't make any deals.

Judge: Case closed. Next party.

(Two days later)

Judge: Oh, no. Here *she* comes again.

Maria: Judge, here I am again.

Judge: I noticed.

Maria: I understand the winter rains will soon start. I must get my soil loosened and the seeds spread —what seeds are left that my neighbor's chickens didn't peck.

Judge: (Gazing off, reflecting) Yes, the rains. Won't they be wonderful? My household helpers have been watering my plot out in the country—using

buckets to carry the water from the spring. I
really have a conscience about hauling all that
weight. But, you know, they want work. They've
got to make ends meet for the extended family.
That one guy's wife is pregnant again.

 At least that won't be your problem. Why don't
you just "count your blessings," knowing that you
won't have any more mouths to feed. Unless of
course. . . . Now that's a way you could make
some money. Don't tell me you can't pay for all
the work I might do for you. Imagine, such effort
on my part, just for a machete and hoe.

Maria: (Looks down, dejected, mute)

Judge: You appear repulsed. Such disrespect for authority, for the bench.

Maria: Tell me, are you a man of justice? I need to
know. What do you say?

Judge: I say you may leave. And quit pestering me.
Do *you* know what that means? People like you
disturb our peace. You make a person weary.

Maria: Oh, are you the weary one? I wonder if we
might share our stories of being weary.

Judge: Not only wearisome. You, a mere widow pre-
sume to address me, a person of status within the
legal system! You persist and think you're some-
body worth my attention. But you waste my time.
Now, be gone! Here sits this important shopkeep-
er—delayed in doing business just because. . . .

(Escribano turns her out. Leaving, Maria calls
back)

Maria: "Just because." Do you hear your own word
—*just*? A bench of justice. Where the just are to

listen. Be assured, I will return."

(Next day)

Maria: My children haven't had food for three days. My boy's getting weak. He could hardly dig, even if I had my hoe and machete. But I am determined to get my tools back. That brother's fields are all planted, so tell him to return them.

Judge: He's not here. How can I? Bring him along.

Maria: You know he wouldn't come with me, on *my* suggestion.

Judge: Then, you're likely the one who's at fault. Persistent. Impatient. You're simply not submissive. And your anger interferes with justice.

Maria: (Hands thrown on what's left of her breasts. Aside) Oh, Mary our Mother, where is mercy? Such reversal of the charges is too much. I know he wants me to give up. Alone, I would. But with you, Comforter, I will not give up. Mary, of the neglected and oppressed, renew my strength to meet those who block justice. . . .

(Continuing) Oh, yes, Judge—

Judge: Woman, you're out of turn. While you were mumbling over there, you lost your place in line. I have time left to hear these three in the *fila* to your left.

Maria: I'm wondering, judge. Do you sleep well at night?

Judge: The question is not proper. But yes! I sleep well—night or day. When you have matters of business to bring before the bench . . . Until then, be gone. Escribano, next case.

(Next day)

Judge: (To himself) Here she is again! As reliable as the sun. Am I to believe she's got enough sense of self that she's not going to give up? I hardly know how else to intimidate her. Her inner strength threatens me. But I can't admit it to her.

Maria: I sense you wish I weren't here.

Judge: For once you understand something!

Maria: I also realize you dislike my courage. Well, I know what justice requires. So I don't easily dismiss unfairness. While I'm here by myself, I also speak for widows as a whole. And I—

Judge: Okay. Okay. I will endure your inconvenience no more. Who is your brother? Where does he live? Get it down for the record. I know what rights are involved. You'll have your tools within two hours. Oh, and, Escribano, add a footnote to this case. For some strange reason, the question, "Will God find faith on earth?" just crossed my mind.

CHAPTER 3

Kingdom, or God's Presence, Order, Will

We have considered peace and justice. We turn now to *kingdom*, meaning God's kingdom and its call for discipleship. Jesus often used the term to describe God's strong presence, God's design for order, or God's will actively done on earth. But because of human experience with kingship—its pageantry, military might, male dominance, wealth, status, or oppressive tactics—we often distort Jesus' meaning. When kingdom suggests to us control without freedom, royal privilege, or human rule, we misunderstand its biblical meaning.

"Kingdom of God" or "Kingdom of Heaven" were ways first-century Jews spoke of their longing for God. Not wanting to desecrate God's name or being, they used other terms, like kingdom. Human systems and institutions and leaders had not brought them well-being for peace is never possible without justice. So the people yearned for divine presence, order, or will. They yearned for salvation or wholeness that would assure all of dignity, equity, and eternal life.

Words like *kingship, rule, realm, govern,* or *lord* suggest ways people organize themselves. Kingdom also suggests boundaries or limits. Kingship reflects how power is exercised. Power—to choose or make decisions. Power—to give or receive authority. Power—to have access to life's basic needs. In most kingdoms a few people gain excess power and use it to exploit the powerless masses.

The concept of God's kingdom begins in the Old Testament. It occurs more often in the four Gospels than in the rest of the New Testament. At first the Israelites accepted Yahweh as "king." They refused to follow other rulers. Against God's preference, Israel later demanded a human king, like their neighbors had. They expected this leader to care for the people within the land and to protect them from external nations or enemies.

God's Order: Distorted or Embraced?

When people rely on human figures or structures, they cease trusting God alone. They fail to understand and pursue God's plan for human relationships. Yet when prophets try to reinstate divine will, they find themselves in conflict with both people of power and subjects who depend on authority figures.

Egotistic human leaders who demand loyalty from followers often fail to insist that God's will be foremost. They fail to distinguish God's will from their own. They oppress. Even their hero, King David, exploited others. Many heroes today also abuse others as they refuse to defer to others or share authority. Leaders who call others to self-sacrifice but deny their pride, or their dependence on high position, misuse authority and distort the concept of servant.

Church structures also absorb into themselves this world's values. Then they support an order that oppresses and dominates. But the Almighty helps people renounce power that harms. Leaders who would implement God's order, will, or presence freely welcome the uniqueness of God's kingdom. It gives status to those with less esteem. It overcomes forces that obstruct the vision of peace and justice.

Powerful people often pacify or alienate others by refusing to admit that they foster injustice. This is what Karl Marx meant when he described religion as "the opiate of the people." Under the guise of upholding religious truth, leaders committed to dominance or economic inequality retain control. They expect deference and submission from others.

But as Jesus' encounter with the cross shows, God's power is present where God seems most absent. We often forget that radical (root) portrayal of kingdom order.

The task for disciples is to let Jesus' teaching and living offer clues to how God organizes and is present among human beings. These clues focus on peace or well-being for all, on mutual empowering. They suggest that Jesus wants to reverse patterns that have "reigned" within nations, churches, structures, and the family.

Those who call for radical discipleship will be rejected for shifting from what has been to what might be. But to follow the Reformer means to insist—gently and firmly—on God's will being done on earth.

Early Christians were a fringe group many resented. Not in agreement with either religious or state officials, they could expect little support.

Yet they persisted. The new dignity transforming the formerly oppressed attracted them. Jesus' priority for the poor and defenseless impressed them. They saw their Teacher radically redefine terms like kingdom, strong and weak, power and powerless. Carrying out God's will as shown by Jesus, they fed the hungry and confronted unfair food systems.

Central to God's kingdom is a new order stripped of sin, a new order cleansed of the desire to dominate.[14] That stirs a basic question, however. "Is the kingdom of God preached by Jesus good news for the poor today?"[15] Have the rifts between human beings—kings versus subjects, rich versus poor, men versus women—caused God's will to be absent from the earth?

If the poor have not been offered good news and God's will is absent from earth, other questions follow.

How have Christ's disciples or churches and

their agencies challenged this? How has the plight of the oppressed been shared? How will the desire to possess be transformed into serving "the least"? Has the church been too strong an ally of the state? Have structures, churches, or individuals shown God's compassion in securing basics for survival and opportunity for everyone to grow?

Such questions are asked to prod, not paralyze. To invite, not impose. The dilemma is a difficult one. But Jesus does not promise ease. He knows and credits our genuine effort. He clearly calls us to persist, rather than resort to making excuses.

We remember again Jesus' keynote message concerning God's coming kingdom (will, order, or presence). He denounced the peoples' desire to gain national triumph through him. He angered them by saying that people with leprosy, widows, and Gentiles—the despised ones—would be more insightful. They would be the ones receptive to God's coming.

Jesus never asked to become the people's human ruler or lordly figure. He presented himself as Healer, as One with the People (Son of Man), as Friend, as the Inclusive One on God's behalf.

Parables of God's Order

Jesus' parables show how God's kingdom differs from standard patterns of human order. When the new image absorbs a person, wholeness emerges. Once reconciled with God, believers are to live out discipleship through justice and peace, or shared love.

If class structure, religious hierarchy, or institutions obstruct, believers are to counter them. When prestige, power, and wealth cause oppression, they must be checked. As disciples work to transform society, all can move toward greater human dignity and salvation.

This will more likely be done through small-scale rather than grand efforts. Even though our social system does not openly promote rigid class distinctions, North American Christians do know different economic and social levels. In subtle or direct ways, we foster this. We can be accountable with others, as with a Sunday school class, to intentionally lessen class divisions.

As trained church employees develop convictions against hierarchy, they could teach that in baptism all are ordained to the sacred task of ministry (telling the good news). Special ordination for the few would cease.

Power is inevitable. But its evil aspect could be transformed through more frequent exchange. The purpose for having it would be to enable those with less to increase their expression of it. This in turn would prompt further exchange by the newly enabled.

Luke's Gospel includes many of Jesus' parables about God's order. A short one compares it with a grain of mustard seed (*Luke 13:18-19; Mark 4:30-32*). Although not the smallest of seeds, about 750 are needed for a gram. Jews confined the plant, which grows rapidly to 8-12 feet, to fields. But the Greeks considered it a garden plant.

The contrast is clear. An insignificant seed becomes a tree in whose branches birds nest, under which they find shade. Hearers would have recalled Old Testament imagery of a tree giving shelter or being a home for a world kingdom (Ezek. 17:22; Dan. 4:9-18).

What a surprise, to think of God's plan for growth involving a mighty tree springing from a speck! That's what a parable does to the ordinary. It reverses what its hearers expect. Many of the people who Israel thought would remain outside or marginal would be included in the great expansion.

Jesus wished to instruct and comfort his followers. He challenged their image of a visible, powerful kingdom, yet offered them hope. Like the seed, seemingly powerless followers would be transformed.

Another parable compares God's kingdom to a woman who took and hid leaven in three measures of meal (*Luke 13:20-21*). Three things surprised the Sabbath hearers: The intentional linking of woman with God's will. The positive treatment of leaven, because it ferments. And the enormous amount of flour (over a bushel) the woman used in a single day's baking.

As they added a portion of dough from the previous day's baking, Palestinian women demonstrated kingdom activity in early Christian communities. Even a little leaven caused a large amount of dough to rise. Here again the ordinary—bread baking—becomes special. Yeast, with its ability to expand what it enters, takes on theological meaning. And the vast quantity of meal used implies a party.[16]

Until the fullness of God's coming, God will be actively present. The process is helped by women who set hidden results into motion. In a sense, they invite people to join the party, to have enough faith to prepare for the final event by reversing this world's values. They expect to entertain God.

Another text uses the metaphor of sheep and goats (*Matthew 25:31-46*). The former—those who attended to the hungry, sick, naked, strangers, or prisoners—were surprised to receive credit.

The "goats" neglected similar opportunity—and then denied they had occasions to serve. Since Jesus dwells unnoticed in the poor, the chance to receive a blessing for deeds done for him may be missed. To fail to do good or to support unfair systems jeopardizes a disciple's status in God's kingdom.

The Pharisees who asked *when* the kingdom of God would come may have expected more than Jesus told them (*Luke 17:20-21*). Jesus offered not a sign to observe, like the moon turning into blood. Not an outward experience. Not something for people to manipulate.

God's order or will functions within. It comes as Jesus asks people to choose or reject God's justice. Because God's order was already present, *when* was the wrong question. Perhaps *who* or *how* would have been more useful. Because no follower was to be subject to another, Jesus was known as King of kings. All believers are kings—and Jesus is their sole King. But because Jesus did not speak or act like a human king, his pattern of inclusive kingship was rejected.

Discipleship Within God's Order

Preparing for God's complete coming includes constant and vigorous discipleship. True discipleship is not limited to good intentions voiced at baptism or short-term promises made at occasional points of renewal.

Luke 14:26-33 gives Jesus' definition of discipleship. Loyalty to God is primary. What may be dear, such as family, must be loved less. Such loyalty means willingness to forego human desires, to choose without condition God the Creator and Sustainer.

This is not liberty to treat relatives irresponsibly. It means not placing commitment to family above commitment to God. It means not defining women by motherhood any more than men by fatherhood. It means that every believer's primary task is to tell others the good news of God's wish to receive all. Every disciple's prime task, to which each is ordained through adult baptism, is to spread God's presence/order/will.

A true disciple chooses friendship with Jesus the Christ. Such a person challenges established norms when these oppose divine principles. Such discipleship may lead to persecution or death, as was the case for early Anabaptists or modern martyrs like El Salvador's Oscar Romero.

Challengers must endure crosses, because God's

will conflicts with patterns that dominate. And when dominant forces (including people) are confronted, they fight back.

For those trained by society to think of themselves as unworthy, discipleship means to claim self-esteem. For those conditioned to be controllers, discipleship calls for self-denial.

Consistent loyalty counts the cost. It knows where radical change is required. We need not make fools of ourselves, however, suggests Luke 14:28-31. Any building project calls for realistic assessment of products needed, principles of engineering, weather factors, and costs. Similarly, anyone going to battle ponders supplies of people, arms, or technology; possible reactions; and long-term strain on resources.

True disciples remain loyal, even when God's cause is unpopular. Trusting God to empower them, they choose to live out Jesus' demands. Knowing that suffering results from faithfulness to Christ, they choose to attack idols of prestige, wealth, male control, and selfish power. Disciples who resist the cross are as useless as salt without flavor.

Another text, *Luke 9:57-62*, notes what is required within God's order for life. We find little support here for three potential followers who make excuses. With self-confidence, a scribe declares that he will follow Jesus no matter where. Jesus reminds him that even lowly foxes and birds have resting places—but not the Son of Man.

Moving from town to town, Jesus found little rest. Rejected, he went on. In endless conflict with powers of evil and interrupted by the multitude, he continually met people in need of saving wholeness. Yet he was homeless. Followers could anticipate similar experience.

When Jesus invited him to follow, another man needed first to bury his father. Whether this meant that the father had already died, or was ill and deserved his son's presence, is unknown. Culture gave absolute priority to the duty of burial. It came before duties of Torah study, temple service, or observing the rite of circumcision.

Even so, Jesus calmly insisted that following God's way was more urgent. The call to proclaim the Eternal dare not be delayed. No other task comes first. Even the request to say farewell first to family implied halfhearted following. Once chosen, a disciple looks forward. Anyone who plows cannot afford to look back. One must give undiverted priority to the divine will and order.

John's account of Jesus' trial also refers to Jesus' kingship (*chapter 18*). Pilate tried to learn if this rabbi pretended to be a messiah, as some Jews charged. While Jesus did not deny kingship imagery, he stressed its nonpolitical, nonearthly, empowering rule.

Although a king, he suffered. When people rejected his radical offer of life, he suffered. When insincere religious people failed to change social injustices, he suffered. Not having done wrong, he was wronged. Insulted, he chose not to retaliate. When tortured, he chose to trust the just Judge. So too are we called to accept the suffering that will

come as we attack injustice in the name of Jesus
the Christ.

A Final Example

The creative piece for this chapter—which reflects on *Luke 18:35-43* and parallel Scriptures—is
presented as a children's story. Pretend the setting
is in India and the main character Bharath, a 30-
year-old blind man who lives about 20 miles from
Modhera.

■ ■ ■

A special festival will soon begin in Modhera.
Lots of people are preparing to go, both from
Bharath's home village and villages farther away.
But Bharath will stay at home. He would like to
join in the celebration. But he's blind. No one
wants to be burdened by him.

Bharath's only choice is to join others from the
village or nearby countryside who are also handicapped. As they sit cross-legged along the roadside each day, they listen to the pilgrims walking
by. They hope the pilgrims will offer a coin or
two. Sometimes those walking by are quiet; the
heat of the day slows them down. At other times
they chatter, call to each other, or chant religious lines.

Bharath especially enjoyed a group of three or
four. They must have run ahead of the adults
traveling with them, then stopped a short dis-
tance from Bharath to wait.

One of the boys was going to the festival for the first time. His enthusiastic friends told him what to expect. Soon each boy gathered a short stick and stones and started digging small holes in the ground for a game. The dust made Bharath sneeze, but the boys didn't notice. They hollered about the rules. They disagreed and complained when someone went out of turn.

Bharath knew they wouldn't give him any *paisa* (coins). They chattered about which sweets they would buy near the temple.

Before long, the adults came near. Hope rose in the row of beggars. The pilgrims expected a special blessing from a priest in Modhera. The beggars expected something from the pilgrims. Giving alms on the way to a festival enhanced a pilgrim's merit. So "haves" and "have nots" served each other a little.

Voices merged or were swallowed in the noise. More sandals shuffled near Bharath. More dust swirled near his face. Bringing his hands together at chest height, then slightly tipping his head, he greeted or pleaded with those passing by. Then he pointed toward a small, torn cloth lying between his two knobby knees. He gently handled the few coins dropped the day before.

The noise level increased. Bharath touched one man's leg, enough to get his attention. "What's going on?" he asked.

"Oh, our special Teacher, Jesus, is not far from us. I guess you can't see him, can you?"

"No, I can't see him, or you, or anyone. But

I've heard others in the village talk about him.
You say he's near?"

"Yes, but he'll never see you, either, with all
this mob."

Oh, yah, thought Bharath. *That's all you know.*
Rarely in his life had he shouted. This was his
chance to try. "Oh, Jesus, Son of David, have
mercy on me!" he hollered.

Those near him snickered. *He doesn't know
how big this crowd is,* they mused.

"Jesus, Son of David, have mercy on me!" he
shouted again.

"Hey, fellah, quit trying to disturb the Master,"
came a response. "Don't you see Jesus is doing
kingdom work?"

"Jesus! Mercy! Mercy!"

Then to everyone's surprise, Jesus heard. Even
more amazing, he stopped—and called for the
crier to come to him. Those who had tried to
stop Bharath's shouts paused in disbelief.

Bharath jumped up from the roadside. Not
even picking up his cloth and coins, he left them
to collect more dust. He needed no second invitation. Two thoughtful pilgrims led him zigzag
through the people to the waiting Teacher.

"What do you want me to do for you?" Jesus
asked. Although he knew, Jesus gave the blind
man a chance to express it himself.

In faith, and with a spirit of deep thanks, the
reply tumbled out of Bharath's mouth: "Master,
let me receive my sight!"

Jesus heard that, too. He understood the blind

man's courage and saw Bharath's trust that Jesus could give sight.

■ ■ ■

Sometimes saying what we think is hard. We have just part of an idea. But if a thoughtful friend encourages us to say even that part, and if she repeats in a kind way what she has heard, the whole idea often becomes clear. That's what "being heard" really means. And Jesus really heard—both Bharath's calls and Bharath's faith that Jesus could heal him. Helping the blind to see is what God's kingdom is all about.

Some people need to see color and brightness and shape. Other people need to see how they mistreat others, or how worthy everyone is in God's sight. We can be sure that Bharath thanked God for his sight by following in the Teacher's way. Will those who ignore needy people, or who prevent their getting help, wake up to see how blind they are?

From Bharath's story we also learn that God *does* hear us. And that we should know what we need from God and what Jesus offers. When we're invited to respond, no one else answers for us. Then our friendship with God grows, through both inner and outer seeing.

CHAPTER 4

Forgiveness, or Redirection

This book suggests that too few people experience well-being or know strength from being justly empowered. Nor does the church clearly envision God's will, presence, and order for relationships. One reason for this is the church's patriarchal, male-dominated understanding of kingdom. The church thus needs forgiveness.

People need links with others and with a Power beyond self. When self-interest overlooks the rights of others, it becomes false god. Then repentance and forgiveness are needed. Until God comes with full peace and justice, the process of forgiveness continues.

Evil domination repeatedly mars relationships of true mutuality and unity. This reduces good power, the power of being enabled. When we forgive others, we redirect the pattern and gain new strength. Through forgiveness each person or group can empower others, rather than experience them as an enemy.

To forgive is to renounce punishing, hurtful behavior. It is to offer mercy and confront injustice. Forgiveness does not ignore or even forget the hurt (lest it be repeated by either party). But it converts or redirects attitudes and actions.[17]

We see examples of the need for such redirection every day. The nation, person, or structure which controls another at the expense of the other's healthy development. Coexistence of poverty and wealth, deprivation and excess opportunity. Labeling classes of people as inferior and superior, "they" and "we," normal and abnormal. All this can change when people repent and forgive.

People who forgive have first been forgiven. With faith in the basic goodness of created humanity, they enter the process. Enabled to have integrity, they encourage growth in others.

On the other hand, to retaliate for wrongs suffered only keeps wounds open. Refusing to admit to or repent of harm done to others blocks full redirection. When memories of a former enemy combine with a sense of that person's worth—in spite of weakness—forgiveness is active.

Latin American Jon Sobrino calls unjust poverty sin.[18] Christian forgiveness within that reality involves taking on the weight of that sin. It means to experience the world of the poor by sharing in poverty and weakness. To forgive is to give voice to the victims or to change structures that oppress and violate people.

"I'm sorry" is often said lightly, with no commitment to redirect behavior that hurts. But evil needs to be transformed into goodness. Genuine forgiveness works at that change.

Jesus' Pattern of Forgiveness

Sobrino notes Jesus' pattern of forgiveness—it is effective for all involved. He "loves the oppressed by being with them and loves the oppressors by being against them . . . offering them salvation by destroying them as sinners."

Believers who repeat Jesus' model prayer, commit themselves "to sharing bread with and working for bread for all those without bread."[19] Exploited people in turn discover their strength, dignity, and contribution to history. With others, they gain the capacity to forgive.

The urge to retaliate for harm done has been present throughout human history. Jesus renounced this and asked for redirection. He invited the oppressed to know self-worth and the oppressors to share privilege.

This, Jesus did at nine meal scenes. Aware of the sacredness of a meal in the ancient world, the Host modeled the power of inclusive table fellowship. Luke's meal texts show a ministry of peace that "builds up an individual's sense of well-being, that ministers forgiveness, reconciliation, and union."[20]

Consider the Last Supper (*Luke 22:14-38*). With Jesus in the large upper room are the Twelve, plus many of the 120 who followed the Teacher before and after the Supper.[21] Grateful to eat his farewell Passover with women and men bonded in a common cause, Jesus drank of the fruit of the vine and broke bread among them. Even toward his enemy, Judas his betrayer, he extended hospitality.

As usual, Jesus used the occasion to teach. Cutting short a dispute, the compassionate Judge nudged any who thought they were great to become as the youngest. And he identified himself with those who modeled service—women.

Earlier (*19:1-10*), Luke told of Jesus' inviting himself to the table of Zacchaeus, the chief toll collector in Jericho, a city that saw many travelers.[22] Zacchaeus, an influential tax collector, showed repentance by feeding many people. For him, redirection meant going far beyond what the law expected. Because he offered no rationalizations, forgiving him must have been a joy.

Zacchaeus' sense of duty led him to offer half his possessions to the poor and to restore fourfold anything wrongfully taken. Religious leaders had set a fifth of what one owned as adequate return. Collectors were to restore double the value taken, but robbers fourfold.

Jesus' offer of salvation—not conquest, political freedom, or reversal of fortune—came in the form of fellowship. He extended friendship and dignity to a man the self-righteous considered unworthy.

God's Pattern of Forgiveness

In *Luke 15:3-32*, human beings are metaphors for God. Three word pictures reveal the divine nature of forgiveness. The shepherd, who searched for the one sheep that was separated from the flock, depicts God. The woman who looks until she finds her lost coin models God. The father who welcomes back a son who was lost reveals God. This in turn led to the need to forgive the resentment an elder son felt his loyalty justified.

When the Pharisees criticized Jesus' ministry of forgiving, of including those they thought outcast, he told these parables. In so doing he also offered his accusers forgiveness for their exclusionary attitudes and practices.

In God's sight all are worthy. Those "sure" of righteousness, who freely rejected others, showed their need for repentance and redirection. Rabbis who refused to eat with the despised of society or to teach the law to women showed how they misunderstood God's kingdom.

In contrast, the godlike shepherd (vv. 3-7) pursued the missing sheep. In either a meadow or wilderness, a lamb could nibble from clump to clump without looking up and be separated from the herd. Then it was defenseless; it had no instinct to find the group. So a shepherd needed to keep alert to and redirect sheep that wandered from the flock.

In a similar way, God wants to draw back people who neglect the purpose for which they were born —to share good news. Since God is in all, no one is hopeless. Whether people choose to be separate, are careless, or are coerced into straying from the Shepherd, they can be redirected.

Jesus wanted to confront religious pride, to invite the self-righteous to see their sin. He also assured them that God would rejoice when they repented.

The godlike woman (vv. 8-10) also searched for

what was lost and celebrated when she found it. Interpreters have minimized her work as mere sweeping, as trivial housekeeping, or picking up because "women tend to lose things."

But her purpose was important. Having lost a tenth (compared to the shepherd's hundredth) of her wealth, she searched—for money, for power in the marketplace, for economic worth, for dignity to survive.

Like God, she deeply wanted to regain what had been hers. Because God loves, she searched until the lost was found. Grieved yet determined, the woman used available resources. With no electricity and perhaps few windows, she brought a lamp. She provided light to penetrate the darkness. She swept thoroughly, not halfheartedly.

God's plan is for people to live redeeming lives. Some who had rejected God repented when they heard Jesus. Whereas this caused the Pharisees disdain, the godlike woman would have rejoiced, Jesus suggests. She, along with friends and angels, celebrate whenever a self-righteous person chooses forgiveness.

In the first two accounts God as shepherd and woman actively searched for what was missing. In the third story (vv. 11-32) God as the father of sons waits with active patience. Penitent sinners felt that God's welcome and inclusion were almost too good to be true. Their opponents did not want to accept the marginal as God's chosen. Yet Jesus persisted in defining faith as surrender to a divine way of loving.

When the younger son discovered that life with pigs and without God was degrading, he returned, repentant, to his parent. He was not prepared for the godlike generosity that welcomed him. His parent offered position (robe), authority (ring), and freedom (shoes).

The elder son, equally unprepared for such generosity, turned bitter. Perhaps he secretly coveted his brother's boldness. Perhaps he had mixed feelings about being loyal in form but not content. Perhaps his call for justice was partially valid.

Each son then, and today's younger and older brothers, must confront themselves. They must decide whether or not to forgive themselves, and accept the forgiveness God stands ready to offer. So Jesus patiently offered a new direction to the religious elite. Denying their privilege, the Pharisees pretended to worship God while being jealous and self-righteous. However, to be correct is not the best image of God's mercy.

How Forgiveness Redirects Peoples' Lives

Luke 5:18-26 tells of the paralytic man at Capernaum. He was a man of faith among friends of faith. The crowded yard and small home where Jesus was teaching did not deter them from getting their friend to the Healer. They hoisted the handicapped man with his cot onto the flat roof. Then they removed some roofing material and lowered him into clear view. No doubt this disturbed many!

Seeing this faith, Jesus declared the man's sins forgiven. That offended the religious leaders. Only

God forgave sins. What blasphemy to claim God's power! Yet they claimed to speak for God through their own strict limits.

Others in the crowd were amazed. This Healer offered more than expected. The man's restored strength and redirected life proved the power of Jesus' forgiveness. Picking up his mat, he went home a grateful soul. Convinced that Jesus was an instrument of God's healing, he had believed and acted on his faith.

An even more scandalous event occurred in the home of Simon (*Luke 7:36-50*). This Pharisee may have had leprosy at one time. He invited quite a few guests, including Jesus. Others passing by were free (in principle) to join them.

One unnamed woman entered with a plan in mind. Jewish women often wore a perfume flask, hung with a cord around the neck. With her hair flowing (a sign of a prostitute), she proceeded to wash, then dry, kiss, and anoint Jesus' feet. She truly ministered to him and his need, perhaps for his coming burial.

That Jesus allowed this disturbed Simon. He must not be a prophet after all. A perceptive person would recognize this dreadful sinner and know that her action defiled the receiver. Programmed as he was, Simon knew what labels went with which people. And this woman had several marks against her even before creating this scene. Compassion personified for this wretched person appalled Simon.

Others present were also stunned. How wasteful! Such treasure should have gone to the poor. How interesting, that the poor are remembered in some situations but so easily forgotten in others. Granted, the alabaster ointment was extravagant. But who condemned the expensive gifts the wise men gave this same Prophet?

Jesus publicly assured the woman of a forgiveness she must already have known. Why, otherwise, would she have shown such devotion? From her fullness of love flowed deep gratitude, which he now reciprocated.

Others offered ample rejection, including Simon. Jesus rebuked Simon's disdain for the woman. As host, he should have offered the guests water to wash their feet. Jesus added a little story about compassion to help Simon get the message.

A creditor had two debtors, neither of which could pay. One owed 500 denarii and the other 50. When the man forgave them both, which was likely the more grateful? Even Simon saw the answer. Yet blinded to the woman, he resented the Master's respect for her. He no doubt also resented Jesus' belief that for years to come what the woman had done would be "told in memory of her." What irony that Simon's attitudes and actions have also left vivid memories of him!

Truly Jesus' freedom to forgive those he considered worthy was hard for biased, religious people to accept, both then and now. Who are we? How is Simon or the woman represented in us?

Another account about forgiveness (*John 7:53-8:11*) has caused controversy through centuries of biblical translation. Was this story part of John's

Gospel or not? We cannot be sure. But we do know that Jesus' forgiveness of the woman's sexual activity, and his condemnation of a double standard for women and men, was consistent with the rest of his ministry. Yet among "Christians" the double standard lives on. The story is retold in poetic form.

One Accused of Adultery

Nameless, a woman without identity,
You appear, dragged by religious accusers.
Scared plus scarred, with reputation marred
You come: defenseless, an easy target for
      abusers.
Interrupting the Teacher—seated, early dawn
Among a crowd gathered to begin a festive day;
Your captors shrewd, intent to slander both you
      and Him
Charge: "This woman . . . caught in the act.
      What do you say?"

There, in the Court of Women,
A pawn, with fate to be decided
By a Stranger, suspect for actions shocking,
Toward wanton sins bold (thought by some
      misguided).
Those presenting you distort the truth.
Pharisees, noted for precision with the Code,
Suggest stoning, the expected for such a *woman*,
Ignoring whether anyone should share the load.
Now who would dare to think a man involved?
Adultery, as with all double standard, difficult
      to ban,

Uniquely to be charged the "weaker sex."
It threatened the property of another *man*.

Delaying a reply, the Teacher doodled,
Writing, who knows what, into the ground.
With finger deft no calligraphy created.
Then, having pondered, without gavel near
       to pound,
He exposed the gravity of the judicial case.
He faulted them for charging without scrutiny
       of self—
"Let the one without sin among you cast
       the first stone."
Then bending to scratch the dust, left each man
       to himself.
Forced by such effrontery, dismayed by turn
       of tide,
Self-righteousness began to leave, not qualified
       to throw.
Beaten in their own intrigue by One prepared
       to pardon
Lone figure: humiliated, deserted, yet destined
       to grow.

Discovering you were left alone, the Teacher
       gently
Proffered: "Neither do I condemn you. Go and
       sin no more."
Shamed more than deserved, you heard the
       freeing judgment.
Accepted, you felt redeemed, to the inner core.
Vulnerable, known for both wounds and
       healing—

Your case dismissed. No scarlet "A" upon your
    breast.
But of the men, those come to do you harm,
Did ever they repent? Did ever *they* apology
    request?

How Enemies, Justice, and Sin Shape Forgiveness

Jesus gave further guidelines for interpersonal
forgiveness in *Luke 6:27-37.* He addressed the love
neighbor/hate enemy tradition of Leviticus 19:17-
18, 33-34 and Exodus 23:4-5. He taught that love
of enemies is strategy, not sentiment.

A negative version of the "golden rule," known
from rabbis and neighbor nations, stated, "What
you do not like, do not to your neighbor." For Israel, neighbor meant Israelite. But Jesus called believers to actively do good, place no fence around
the term *neighbor*—and expect no favor in return.

Purposes of forgiveness are clear. To free enemies from hate or brokenness. To prove one's own
love by refusing revenge. To bring guilty offenders
to repentance. To conquer evil with good.

Jesus gives examples. If someone strikes one side
of your jaw, offer the other side. If someone takes
your outer garment (often used by the poor for a
cover at night) give also your undershirt. If someone begs or steals your goods, do not expect the
items to be returned.

While such examples are useful, often those who
endure the brunt of sin are already demeaned. Too
many physically abused wives turn the second
cheek to a hurtful husband who never repents.

People with more clothing than needed fail to admit the effect of greed on those with just one tunic. Few of us with multiple choices, honored positions, extra housing or food confess how our imbalance steals from those with less.

Such awareness need not cause Christians to despair. Or to do nothing since full equity is unlikely. To be more sensitive than a year ago, or to repent more convincingly is part of the process. Forgiveness and justice do go together. Since evil causes harm, we cannot approve it. A person unwilling to repent is not to be excused. That encourages injustice. Forgiveness which does not cause change also affects the person's relationship with God.

What Jesus addresses here is attitude. Hearers must face injury without desiring revenge. They are to offer love. But to forgive enemies will sometimes anger them more. To love is to confront evil. While the promise of reversal in "God's good time" can sustain victims of injustice, that truth dare never lead to endorsing oppression.

Jesus' new teaching about forgiveness in the Sermon on the Mount forbade retaliation. Several Old Testament passages still practiced permitted a hurtful response. "He who kills a man shall be put to death . . . fracture for fracture, eye for eye, tooth for tooth . . . (Lev. 24:17-21).

Jesus' radical shift to "love your neighbor" expanded the meaning of both *neighbor* and *love*. Anyone is a neighbor. Any needy person deserves care. This may mean confronting institutions and systems that cause injustice. Or stopping practices that destroy others and therefore one's own self.

Luke 17:3-4 teaches more about forgiveness. Sin —the will to dominate others or to assume authority belonging to God alone—always has consequences. Sin is against the Creator and creation. The power or energy needed to repent or to forgive is also divine.

In interpersonal relations, we are to forgive, as often as needed, an offender who repents. We are to be neither indifferent to evil nor prone to hold grudges. Neither to forgive nor to request forgiveness is a sign of weakness. But both, if genuine, involve effort. Since sin is not to be overlooked, the guilty one is to be rebuked—in love. True love wants the guilty person to move to confession so that forgiveness can take place.

Often all parties involved in troubled relationships need to repent—to ask for and receive pardon. All need to acknowledge each other's truth. Usually, the ones with advantage (position or status, more verbal skill, wealth) find confession more difficult. The more oppressed then carry additional blame if forgiveness does not emerge.

This burden becomes especially heavy when those who judge the situation are not free to fault a "hero" or believe an "underdog." Our complicity in such patterns calls all of us to repent and forgive.

Matthew's text gives less credit to waiting for one to repent before forgiveness is offered. Otherwise the cycle could become endless.

Benefits to the forgiver are worth noting. At times a person refuses to rebuke another to avoid breaking Jesus' principle about the mote and beam.

Even so, sin needs to be named. Sometimes forgiveness brings the other to repent. Sometimes the pattern of injustice is so subtle or entrenched that there is no humility and ownership for sin. Victims of such circumstances hardly deserve further blame if they wait to forgive.

Further caution is appropriate. Sin clouds a persons viewpoint. We can convince ourselves that we are only victims when in fact we share responsibility for broken relationships. We need to face personal flaws as surely as address another's.

Forgiveness Against Odds

Examples of forgiveness appear in *Revolutionary Forgiveness*. This book was written by thirteen North Americans after living and learning in Nicaragua.[23] Following the 1979 Triumph, the new Minister of the Interior, Tomas Borge, visited the imprisoned leaders of Somoza's National Guard. These prisoners had tortured and murdered up to 50,000 Nicaraguans during the insurrection.

On one visit Comandante Borge recognized the guardsman who had tortured him. "What are you going to do to me? What is your revenge?" asked the prisoner. Borge responded by extending his hand and saying, "I forgive you. That is my revenge."[24]

Although he could not forget the pain of torture, Borge invited the man into right relation with him and the revolutionary movement. He recognized the oppressor as victim of a system and hoped forgiveness would prevent further violence.

Another report describes the process of forgiveness. A woman whose son had been killed was asked how she manages without hatred.

> "I don't hate, but I won't hug them [the counter-revolutionaries] either. . . . We don't hate but we have to defend ourselves. . . . We want to live, to work in peace. . . . They are killing entire families . . . innocent, unarmed people . . . this has no forgiveness."[25]

This woman's attitude remains contradictory. But even such contradictions, which show honest wrestling, can gradually lead to redirection.

Since forgiveness affects all of an experience, parts of it dare not be blocked out or erased. The wrongness or injury in a relationship needs to be owned by each for forgiveness to occur. A first step in the process is "for both parties to be willing to admit to and dispose of the injury that has been done. . . . There is no forgiveness apart from justice."[26]

In radical forgiveness, not only individuals need to change. Systems (such as family) and structures (like church boards or institutions), can have built-in injustices. For example, men in the family or church may hold undue power. Such patterns must change for everyone to experience justice.[27]

According to *Luke 23:34, 39-43*, Jesus spoke an important truth just prior to his death. Luke probably owes this firsthand report to the faithful women. As the Despised hangs between two thieves, Luke's Jesus utters, "Father, forgive them; for they know not what they do."

Here Jesus' love rises above his suffering. Many who wished to crucify him were not aware of the Son of God. Soldiers were expected to carry out orders. Without wrath, the Crucified cares for his enemies rather than asking God to punish them. What powerful and creative forgiveness!

Probably overhearing Jesus' exchange from the cross, the two thieves responded quite differently. One was sarcastic. "Are you not the Christ? Save yourself and us!"

Hearing no fear of the Almighty in him, the other thief rebuked the first. And having heard enough to know that Jesus did not deserve what all three were facing, he repented and asked a favor. Understanding that Jesus' death would not be final, he asked the Redeemer to remember him in the future kingdom (order/presence).

That penitent one did not have long to wait. Jesus forgave him even as together they hung on their crosses. That day he knew wholeness. So today, women and men who share Jesus' suffering are assured of peace, justice, and forgiveness in the Creator's unique kingdom.

A Final Example

In this chapter, we connected meal-eating with forgiveness. We conclude with Luke's first meal scene (*Luke 5:27-39*). A few paragraphs first describe the biblical episode. Then several possible statements of confession from different characters are offered. Imagine the setting as El Salvador, Central America. Characters include a toll collector Mario, a few religious Pharisees or scribes, the invited guests, and Jesus.

■ ■ ■

Near Quezaltepeque, a city where travelers were stopped for roadside customs, Jesus talked with Mario the collector. Since Mario had already heard about the Teacher and was interested in him, Mario didn't hesitate when Jesus called, "Follow me."

As Mario thought of friends he had met along the road or in business, he decided to invite a hundred of them for a meal on his patio. They would see for themselves what this radical one was like.

Although the guests were mostly from groups avoided by the "religious types," Jesus didn't mind. He and his followers that day were ready for a fiesta. They ate together. They exchanged friendship and accepted each other. They seemed to enjoy meeting oxen drivers, butchers, barbers, and collectors of assorted government taxes. This would be Mario's last show of wealth.

Interrupting the casual guests, a few priests and writers of religious papers stormed the fiesta. They weren't very subtle about spying.

The talk became heated as they criticized Jesus. "Why do you revel with these rascals? Don't you realize how defiled you get when you mix with people who don't know or keep the laws? To eat with such sinners shames you and your disciples. It makes us doubt your honesty, too."

The radical one absorbed the charges. He noted their self-righteous attitudes. Knowing they wouldn't admit to any need, Jesus turned to the "needy ones." He praised them for readiness to repent. They were his kind of people. The priests could undermine themselves, if they chose to do so. The Forgiver wished everyone would receive his offer; only some were redirected.

Some thought Jesus' followers should be more like other religious folk. For example, they should fast and pray more. But that would have been like God's asking wedding guests to avoid food when they joined the meal's Host. Or like mixing what doesn't go together—oil and water, sweet water and lemonade, new and old. Neither part of the mix is wrong. Forgiveness is simply not possible in the mixture.

Prayers of Confession

From Mario:

> Forgiving One, thanks for joining us at my table. That You receive us who are not accepted by religious types says more than You could teach in hours. Your pleasure in this fiesta says that joy is an integral part of life. Guide us to include others more consciously, to celebrate Your presence more often. Amen.

> True Guide, Your direct invitation to follow You compels me. I'm sorry You and Your way haven't always led me in the past. But convinced that my

past actions—whether dishonest or unjust—will be pardoned, I join Your crowd. I leave my trade of collecting taxes to follow Your way of dignity and life. Keep me from reverting to old patterns. Amen.

Friend of Sinners, I come to You remembering the travelers I took advantage of, the times I added a metal ball to the scales. You know how I used the extra money. Although my supervisors never knew how much I charged, little escaped Your eye. Assure me of Your love, and I will befriend those who journey with and without You. In Your sacred name.

From Pharisees and Scribes:

God of Sinners, You know those who fail to keep the law. And You know us who keep it faithfully, who rise above sin. Why should we ask for help? But just in case . . . what was that about "pride going before a fall"? Stand tall with us. Amen and Amen and Amen.

Rabbi, we note a different pattern in You. While our synagogues have been open to sinners, we leaders would never go out to invite them to join us. If You trust us to change our former ways, we pledge ourselves to take the initiative. We want to overcome the arrogance that discredits "marginal" folk. Be with us in our gestures. Make them genuine— now and forever. Amen.

(A brief dialogue of confession)
Leader: Let us admit who we have been.
Pharisees: We are the separate ones. We devoted ourselves to ceremonial cleanness, to scant tolerance for those who we thought were unclean.

Scribes: We kept the record straight—so straight we became bent out of shape.

Leader: Let us strive to be new people.

Pharisees: We will not use a new shirt to patch old shirts. Because both cutting into the new one or washing the old one with a new patch destroys the fabric.

Scribes: We will use only new bags for our drink. We will not retain old patterns for new vision.

Leader: So be it.

From Banquet Guests:

Guest of Guests, we greet You with awe, yet we know You wish to be near us. We have kept You at arms length. Now draw us to You as we are drawn to our neighbors. Help us mend our fences or stone walls as we tear down the barriers that have divided us. Teach us to receive those who reject us. Eat with us and with them as a sign of our mutual redirection. Forgiven, we forgive.

Conclusion

This book has attempted to use New Testament Scripture (primarily Luke) to urge the creation of peace and justice. Since wholeness and mutual empowerment are basic principles of biblical truth, no one should be deprived of them. To do so is to sin—against neighbor, Creator, self. And that requires forgiveness.

Through teaching and example, the Prince of Peace and enabler of justice outlined God's good order. Jesus' inaugural address (Luke 4:16ff.), which combined the priestly and prophetic, clarifies his mission to the poor or underclass. Body, mind, and spirit are to be healed and enlightened. Vengeance and injustice must be confronted whether among people, structures, or systems.

I encourage readers to find resources that expand on what I have begun here. Noteworthy are *Shalom: The Bible's Word for Salvation, Justice, and Peace*, by Perry B. Yoder, and *To Change the World: Christology and Cultural Criticism*, by Rosemary Radford Ruether.[28]

Yoder declares that biblical peace is "squarely against injustice and oppression." Shalom is "abolishment of structures of oppression and violence."[29]

Ruether clearly defines kingdom.

> The kingdom, for whose coming Jesus taught us to pray, is defined quite simply as "God's will done on earth." God's will done on earth means the fulfillment of people's basic human physical and social needs: daily bread, remission of debts, which includes both the wrongs that we have done others, and also the financial indebtedness that holds the poor in bondage to the rich, avoidance of the temptations that lead us to oppress one another, even in God's name, and finally, deliverance from evil.[30]

I have discussed forgiveness and its connection to achieving peace and justice. I had hoped to study Luke's texts on the theme of *servant* but ran out of space. New, creative work with that biblical concept is also needed if people are to find authentic, empowered well-being.

May all of us hear more convincingly Jesus' clear call to justice.

Notes

1. Texts in order of appearance (from Luke except those in parentheses).

Peace	Justice	Kingdom	Forgiveness
9:51-56	4:16-30	13:18-19	22:14-38
10:25-37	(Isa. 61)	13:20-21	19:1-10
17:11-19	1:46-55	(Matt. 25:31-46)	15:3-7,
10:38-42	12:13-21	17:20-21	8-10,
12:51-53	14:12-14,	14:26-33	11-32
14:26-27	15-24	9:57-62	5:18-26
6:6-11	16:19-31	(John 18)	7:36-50
13:10-17	9:28-43	18:35-43	(John 7:53—8:11)
14:1-6	20:45—21:4		6:27-37
19:45-46	11:42-44		17:3-4
22:35-38, 49-53	18:9-14		23:34, 39-43
23:1-5, 13-25	18:2-5		5:27-39
21:10-19			
8:43-48			

2. Bruce C. Birch, "Old Testament Foundations for Peacemaking in the Nuclear Era," *The Christian Century*, December 4, 1985, p. 1116.

3. Alan Richardson, ed. *A Theological Wordbook of the Bible* (New York: Macmillan Co.), 1951, p. 165.

4. Robert McAfee Brown, *Theology in a New Key*. Responding to Liberation Themes (Delhi: Lithouse Publications, 1983, p. 91).

5. Sharon D. Welch, *Communities of Resistance and Solidarity: A Feminist Theology of Liberation* (New York: Orbis/Maryknoll), 1985, p. 47.

6. Sergio Torres and Virginia Fabella, eds. *The Emergent Gospel: Theology from the Underside of History* (New York: Orbis/Maryknoll), 1978, p. 241.

7. Brown, *Theology in a New Key*, p. 96.

8. Welch (expanding on Rosemary Radford Ruether's thought in *New Woman/New Earth*, p. 83), p. 68.

9. Rosemary Radford Ruether, "Feminist Spirituality and Historical Religion," *Harvard Divinity Bulletin*, February-March, 1986, p. 7.

10. Abraham J. Heschel, *The Prophets* Vol. II (New York: Harper & Row), 1962, p. 264.

11. Jon Magnuson, "Affirming Native Spirituality: A Call to Justice," *The Christian Century*, December 9, 1987, p. 1115.

12. Robert McAfee Brown, *Unexpected News: Reading the Bible with Third World Eyes* (Philadelphia: Westminster Press), 1984, p. 83.

13. Ibid., p. 84.

14. Ruether, p. 6.

15. George V. Pixley, "Biblical Embodiments of God's Kingdom: A Study Guide for the Rebel Church" (from Harvey Cox's forward to Pixley's *God's Kingdom: A Guide for Biblical Study*), in *The Bible and Liberation: Political and Social Hermeneutics*, edited by Norman K. Gottwald (New York: Orbis/Maryknoll), 1983, p. 110.

16. I wish to acknowledge insight into these two parables from Mary Schertz' two research papers for a Greek Exegesis course at Associated Mennonite Biblical Seminaries: "The Parable of the Mustard Seed, Mark 4:30-32" and "The Parable of the Leaven, Matthew 13:33 and Luke 13:20-21," October/November 1982.

17. Some of this introductory material has been gathered from various writers in the *Concilium* volume titled *Forgiveness*, edited by Casiano Floristan and Christian Duquoc (Edinburgh: T. & T. Clark Ltd.), 1986.

18. Ibid., Jon Sobrino, "Latin America: Place of Sin and Place of Forgiveness," pp. 45-56.

19. Ibid., p. 53 and George Soares-Prabhu, " 'As We Forgive' Interhuman Forgiveness in the Teaching of Jesus," p. 59.

20. Josephine Massyngbaerde Ford, "Cursing and Blessing as Vehicles of Violence and Peace in Scripture," in *Peace in a Nuclear Age: The Bishops' Pastoral Letter in Perspective*, edited by Charles J. Reid, Jr. (Washington, D.C.: Catholic University of America Press), 1986, p. 32.

21. See Quentin Quesnell, "The Women at Luke's Supper," in R. Cassidy and P. Scharper, eds., *Political Issues in Luke-Acts* (New York: Orbis/Maryknoll), 1983, pp. 59-79.

22. See J. Massyngbaerde Ford, *My Enemy Is My Guest: Jesus and Violence in Luke* (New York: Orbis/Maryknoll), 1984, pp. 76-78.

23. The Amanecida Collective, *Revolutionary Forgiveness: Feminist Reflections on Nicaragua* (New York: Orbis/Maryknoll), 1987.

24. Ibid., p. 83.

25. Ibid., p. 84.

26. Ibid., p. 93.

27. Ibid., p. 102.

28. Perry B. Yoder, *Shalom: The Bible's Word for Salvation, Justice, and Peace* (Newton, Kan: Faith and Life Press), 1987. Rosemary Radford Ruether, *To Change the World: Christology and Cultural Criticism* (New York: Crossroad), 1981.

29. Yoder, p. 6.

30. Ruether, *To Change the World*, p. 15.

For Further Study

In addition to the resources listed in the *Notes*, you are encouraged to consult the following sources.

Brueggemann, Walter. *Living Toward a Vision: Biblical Reflections on Shalom*. Philadelphia: United Church Press, 1976.

Cassidy, Richard J. *Jesus, Politics, and Society: A Study of Luke's Gospel*. New York: Orbis/Maryknoll, 1978.

France, R. T. "Liberation in the New Testament." *Evangelical Quarterly*, V. viii, No. 1, January 1986, pp. 3-23.

Lee-Pollard, Dorothy A. "Powerlessness as Power: A Key Emphasis in the Gospel of Mark." *Scottish Journal of Theology*, V. 40, pp. 173-188.

Ringe, Sharon H. *Jesus, Liberation, and the Biblical Jubilee: Images for Ethics and Christology*. Philadelphia: Fortress Press, 1985.

Sobrino, Jon. *Jesus in Latin America*. New York: Orbis/Maryknoll, 1987.

Swidler, Leonard. *Biblical Affirmations of Woman*. Philadelphia: Westminster Press, 1979.

Tamez, Elsa. *Bible of the Oppressed*. New York: Orbis/Maryknoll, 1982.

I also want to credit ideas useful for this study from the *Interpreter's Bible* Luke/John, V. viii, and Gospel of Luke commentaries by E. Earle Ellis, Norval Geldenhuys, F. Godet, R. C. H. Lenski, I. Howard Marshall, and Leon Morris.

The Author

Dorothy Yoder Nyce is a writer, teacher, and volunteer. She is also parent, with John, of college-age daughters Lynda and Gretchen. She has been a justice activist within the Mennonite Church for fifteen years. Her prime focus has been justice for women—in the church, in Scripture interpretation, in the recording of history, and in global concerns.

Dorothy was born and raised in Kalona, Iowa. She gained respect for disciplined biblical study from her parents, who were longtime, adult Sunday school teachers.

A 1960 graduate of Goshen College (Indiana), she completed in 1981 the M.Div. degree at Associated Mennonite Biblical Seminaries (Indiana).

She taught part-time at these schools and currently teaches Bible and Sexuality at Goshen College.

A board member of the Mennonite Board of Missions since 1983, Dorothy chairs the Overseas Divisional Committee. She is a teaching/preaching elder at Assembly Mennonite Congregation in Goshen. During the 1970s, as a member of the MCC Peace Section, she helped found its Task Force on Women.

Dorothy edited two books: *Which Way Women?* (1980) and *Weaving Wisdom: Sermons by Mennonite Women* (1983). Writer of numerous articles in church papers, she also wrote 12 articles for *The Mennonite Encyclopedia, Volume V.*

During 1987 she helped create a slide set and video, *Women of Strength: Ancient [Proverbs 31] and Modern [global].*

The Nyces lived in India at three different times. Dorothy returned there with a Fulbright study group in 1988 and consulted with two international, Christian schools in 1990. She presented the C. Henry Smith lectureship at several Mennonite colleges in 1989 and developed her focus of justice issues into the book *Strength, Struggle and Solidarity: India's Women.*

PEACE AND JUSTICE SERIES

Edited by J. Allen Brubaker and Elizabeth Showalter

This series of books sets forth briefly and simply some important emphases of the Bible regarding war and peace and how to deal with conflict and injustice. The authors write from within the Anabaptist tradition. This includes viewing the Scriptures as a whole as the believing community discerns God's Word through the guidance of the Spirit.

Some of the titles reflect biblical, theological, or historical content. Other titles in the series show how these principles and insights are practical in daily life.

The books in this series are published in North America by:

Herald Press
616 Walnut Avenue
Scottdale, PA 15683
USA

Herald Press
490 Dutton Drive
Waterloo, ON N2L 6H7
CANADA

For overseas distribution or permission to translate, write to the Scottdale address listed above.

BS2595.6.5 N93 19 0   c.1
Nyce, Dor thy Yoder   100105 000
Jesus' cle r c ll to justice /

3 99 0 00085257 2
GOSHEN C LLEGE-GOOD LIBRARY